THE GREAT
2030 EXPOSED!

M000211941

Vaccine Passports & 5G Microchips, COVID-19
Mutations or The Next Pandemic?

WEF Agenda – Build Back Better - The Green Deal
Explained

Rebel Press Media

Disclaimer

Our other books

Check out our other books for other unreported news, exposed facts and debunked truths, and more.

Join the exclusive Rebel Press Media Circle!

You will get a new updates about the unreported reality delivered in your inbox every Friday.

Sign up here today:

https://campsite.bio/rebelpressmedia

Introduction

*All of humanity is subjected to biggest and most
dangerous scientific experiment ever*

Back in the spring, a possible link between 5G and the
coronavirus was dismissed in the media as a conspiracy
theory. However, a team of Italian, American and
Russian scientists has published a study in which they
show that 5G does indeed turn human skin cells into a
large antenna. The electromagnetic 5G millimeter
waves can be transmitted by the skin cells to other cells,
thus playing an important role in the production of the
coronavirus.

5G allows virus-like structures to be built into human cells

In "5G technology and incorporation of coronavirus into
skin cells," the scientists point out that human DNA
consists of charged electrons and atoms, and has an
inductor-like structure. Inductors respond to external
electromagnetic waves, and also move and produce
some additional waves inside the cells.

These waves are similar to the hexagonal and pentagonal bases of their DNA source. These waves produce a number of holes in fluids within the nucleus (cell nucleus). To fill these gaps, additional hexagonal and pentagonal bases are produced, which can combine with each other and form virus-like structures such as coronavirus.

To produce these viruses in a cell, it is necessary that the wavelength of the external waves be shorter than the size of the cell. In this way, 5G millimeter waves may be a good candidate to build virus-like structures such as Covid-19 in human cells.

All of humanity subjected to the largest experiment ever

5G producers say that the high frequency beams are too weak to penetrate the human body, and that there is no hard scientific evidence of any major adverse effects on our health.

However, the circumstantial scientific evidence is piling up, but is not (yet?) accepted, most likely because of large commercial interests, and presumably also because 5G is part of an ideological and geopolitical agenda to bring the entire world population under total control.

With 5G in combination with hastily developed, barely tested but already purchased corona vaccines, the whole of humanity is without a doubt exposed to the biggest and by far the most dangerous scientific experiment ever, and that with the consent of almost all governments. So in this respect, too, our society is actually being turned into one big concentration camp.

What constitutes a virus?

That a virus is not a living organism, but merely a packet of DNA/RNA information - which thus indeed seems to be able to be activated or affected by external electromagnetic waves.

'DNA or RNA without a host cell is like a body without a brain. It is dead. It does and cannot do anything. Nor can it survive. Encapsulated in protein, it could still float from A to B, but it can only do so in complete darkness. In minuscule UV light, the DNA or RNA is gone and it breaks down.'

Table of Contents

Chapter 1: The rollout

Governments want to push 5G through because it allows citizens to be tracked and monitored 24/7/365

The number of scientists who have major reservations about the introduction of 5G is steadily growing. The British epidemiologist Professor John William Frank of the University of Edinburgh is calling for the rollout of 5G worldwide to be suspended for the time being, until it has been independently confirmed and proven that the technology is safe and poses no danger to health Until now, governments have relied almost exclusively on studies by (or sponsored by) the big Tech companies, and of course they will never put their billion-dollar profits at risk by rejecting their own products.

Professor Frank is not against 5G, but he does think that far too little research has been done on it. That's why he argues that it's better to err on the side of caution, and freeze the rollout of the new mobile data traffic systems for now.

There are a lot more antennae and a lot more EMF radiation.

Frank, like many other academics, writes in the Journal of Epidemiology & Community Health that the primary threat of 5G is the massive antenna density required for these extremely high frequencies. Every few lampposts, a new antenna must be placed, exposing people to even more electromagnetic radiation (EMF). A federal commission of specialists in the United States has acknowledged the health harm that existing networks such as 4G and WiFi can cause.

Despite this, almost no credible epidemiological research on the impact of 5G on human health have been undertaken, according to the professor. Furthermore, 5G employs not just considerably higher frequencies, but also an entirely new supporting technology to handle massive volumes of data. For 5G to work, billions of antennas and signal amplifiers must be put every 100 to 300 meters around the planet. Amazon's upcoming 3,236 5G satellites, as well as the 12,000 to 30,000 Elon Musk plans to deploy into orbit, will soon cover areas where antennas are not conceivable.

'A rising number of worldwide engineers, scientists, and doctors are urging countries to raise their RF-EMF safety standards, commission more and better research, and halt further public exposure increases until there is stronger evidence that it is safe.'

The precautionary principle dictates that 5G deployment be halted.

Professor Frank isn't convinced that 5G and other EMFs are damaging to health and the environment, despite the fact that the WHO and a slew of tech experts assert otherwise. He believes that the spread of 5G should be halted immediately due to the "precautionary principle." You should not take any unnecessary chances when it comes to human health. That premise should be sufficient grounds to 'declare a ban on that (5G) exposure, pending adequate scientific inquiry into the alleged health risks.'

He goes on to explain that there is no compelling need to roll out 5G at a rapid speed in terms of public health and safety. It is being done primarily because the new technology will provide a significant boost to the Big Tech industry. With the existing 4G network, consumers have no shortage of rapid mobile data connections.

Governments want 5G to be implemented as soon as possible in order to have complete global control.

Frank neglects to add that governments are just as invested in 5G as the tech and media behemoths. The Bill & Melinda Gates Foundation and the Pentagon's technology development arm, DARPA, have teamed up with the tech firm Profusa to develop an implantable nanotech biosensor made of hydrogel (a substance similar to a soft contact lens) that can be injected alongside a vaccine and applied just beneath the skin, where it actually merges with your body. All information about yourself, your body, and your health may be controlled remotely thanks to the nanotech component.

As a result, 5G enables a global totalitarian control system that dictatorships of the past could only dream of. It will allow anyone's location, movements, and actions - and, in the not-too-distant future, thoughts and emotions - to be tracked, monitored, and manipulated 24 hours a day, seven days a week, while all personal information, such as vaccination status and bank balances, will be instantly accessible. Countless surveillance cameras with facial recognition and social-credit status checks are linked to this system, as is the Microsoft system (with patent no. 2020-060606) that converts your own body into a means of payment (and ID/vaccination proof) that is already in the testing phase.

According to some, a distance of at least one and a half meters is required for this system to function correctly, because signals can be disrupted if bodies are too close together. It's unclear whether this is true, but without social distancing, surveillance cameras (and even smartphones) will have a much harder time scanning all foreheads in a crowded crowd in real time for the presence of the fluorescent M-Neongreen / Luciferase enzyme, the injected mark that in the future could serve as proof that you've been properly vaccinated and thus have access to society.

Is there a conspiracy theory?

Given that multiple scientists and other professionals have stated for months that 1.5 meters makes no difference in the alleged transmission of a virus, it's past time for more people to wonder why "social separation" must continue to be enforced unabatedly. Unfortunately, certain odd conspiracy theories, such as that 5G would trigger the coronavirus, and terrible deeds, such as setting fire to transmission towers, have polluted real concerns to 5G (intentionally?).

Politicians, the tech industry, and all mainstream media and magazines that rely on one another in any way invariably claim that these are all debunked "conspiracy theories," but when even the venerable Scientific American published an article on October 17, 2019, with the headline "We have no reason to believe that 5G is safe - Contrary to what some people say, there may be health risks,"

Chapter 2: 5G nanotech biosensors

'Implantable 5G nanotech biosensor as early as 2021 in Covid-19 vaccines' Humanity evolving into transhuman in future is integrated with global digital control system.

DARPA, the Pentagon's technology development arm, and the Bill and Melinda Gates Foundation are working with Profusa to develop an implanted nanotech biosensor constructed of hydrogel (substance similar to a soft contact lens). This biosensor, which is about the size of a grain of rice, is injected with a vaccine and placed just beneath the skin, where it blends in with your body. Through 5G, the nanotech component enables remote monitoring of all information about yourself, your body, and your health.

The FDA is likely to approve the biosensor, which can also receive information and commands, in early 2021, just in time for the planned global Covid-19 vaccine campaign.

In March, DefenseOne reported on a hydrogel biosensor that is "inserted underneath the skin with a hypodermic needle." It contains, among other things, a specifically engineered molecule that emits a fluorescent signal once the body begins to fight an infection. This signal is detected by the electronic component attached to (/in) the skin, which subsequently transmits a warning to a doctor, a website, or a government agency. 'It's basically a skin-based blood lab that can detect the body's response to disease even before other signs like coughing appear.'

All physiological processes are monitored by biosensors and transmitted over 5G.

The biosensor will not be perceived as an intruder by the body and attacked as a result of its use of hydrogel, but will instead integrate with it. The sensor can also track your hormone levels, heart rate, respiration, body temperature, sex life, emotions, and anything else, according to the manufacturer. All of this data will soon be delivered to every medical and government authority via 5G.

Profusa is now working on a study with Imperial College, which was made famous by its ludicrous forecasts of doom over Covid-19, which were quickly proven to be completely false. Lockdowns, social isolation, and the related partial collapse of the economy, as well as the removal of many civil liberties, were all founded on these.

Transhuman human being is integrated with global digital control system

The biosensor, which may therefore be incorporated into Covid-19 vaccines as early as 2021, comes very close to realizing the aspiration of a transhuman human, in which everyone is totally controllable and even steerable. The 'new human', or the human 2.0 as envisioned by the tech elite around Bill Gates and Elon Musk, will be gradually transformed into a kind of cyborg between now and 2025-2030, and become an integral - and therefore irreversible - part of a global digital control system, in which personal freedoms will have completely disappeared, and even human free will will will have been taken away.

Chapter 3: Vaccine Passport Protests

More than 70 parliamentarians rally against this 'heinous trap'

In an open letter to Prime Minister Boris Johnson, more than 1,200 British Christian leaders asked him not to adopt testing and vaccination passports.

In fact, they label it "the most dangerous proposition ever" since it amounts to "an unethical form of pressure" to force people to be Covid-19 tested or vaccinated.

Various denominations, including Anglican and Catholic, have leaders in the church. They believe that test and vaccine passports are the precursor to a "surveillance state," a totalitarian control state, and that they will put an end to what is left of liberal democracy.

The government in London maintains that no final decision has been reached, but all indicators point to these test/vaccination passports arriving soon, just as they did in Europe.

They will initially be marketed as a passport to more 'freedom' (catering, events, shopping, etc.), but as they become more prevalent, the standards will become increasingly strict, eventually eliminating untested and unvaccinated people from society entirely.

'Medical Apartheid' is a term used to describe a system of medical discrimination.

According to church leaders, such passports result in "medical apartheid... It establishes a surveillance state in which the government controls certain parts of citizens' life through technology. Over the course of a few years, that 'certain' threatens to be expanded to ALL areas.

'This is one of the most hazardous policy ideas ever made in the history of British politics,' warn church leaders, who emphasise that they will never deny those without such a passport access to their churches, regardless of the government's decision.

'Discrimination' and 'horrific trap' are two words that come to mind.

More than 70 British legislators openly protested the planned test/vaccination passports earlier this month. They claim that needing to show such proof in order to enter a pub, for example, is discriminatory. It also creates further societal divisions. (In any case, the West's entire approach is based on 'divide and rule.')

Conservative MP Steve Baker even termed these passports "a nasty trap." Labour leader Sir Keir Starmer expressed "great alarm" over this looming new form of discrimination.

Chapter 4: Killer jabs?

Low concentrations of spike protein have already changed the respiratory and immunological systems of vaccinated people - Indications that vaccinated people may be a hazard to unvaccinated individuals are becoming stronger –

A government that cares about your health would suspend vaccinations right away.

Criticism of the Covid-19 vaccines is also swelling from established active science.

Dr. Lee Makowski, chair of the bioengineering department at Northeastern University, warns in the journal Viruses that there is growing evidence that the spike protein, which is produced by the human body at the instruction of ALL corona vaccines, can cause major health damage and even death.

Politicians, media, and agencies such as the CDC and the WHF claim that the spike protein is "harmless," and the Covid vaccines that cause the body to produce this protein are "safe.

However, a growing number of established active scientists are seeing more and more evidence and proof that just the opposite is true.

'Damage, serious infections and death from these vaccines?'

The title of Dr. Makowski's article in the journal Viruses says it all:

'Do Covid vaccines designed to create immunity to the spike protein instead cause harm, serious infections and death?'

The researchers found that even at low concentrations, the spike protein induces genetic changes in the respiratory tract, and directly affects the immune system's response to inflammation and viruses. In fact, according to Dr. Makowski, it seems that only the spike protein is responsible for the now infamous blood clots, rather than the (supposed) SARS-CoV-2 virus itself.

If this is confirmed by more scientists, then the Covid-19 vaccines - which regardless of their mode of action (mRNA, adenovirus/viral vector, DNA) all code for the spike protein - are even more dangerous to human health than critical scientists have already suspected since last year.

Are vaccinated people becoming walking infection hotspots?

Moreover, it is becoming plausible that Dr. Lee Merritt may well be right, and the spike protein produced in vaccinated people is transmissible to others. In other words, vaccinated people become walking spike factories, and thus could also infect unvaccinated people with a harmful, potentially deadly autoimmune disease.

Scientists at the Sloan Kettering Institute sound another, equally dire warning: the mRNA in the vaccines can cause proteins that prevent the development of cancer to be suppressed. Thus, the Covid vaccines increase the risk of getting cancer.

UCLA Dr. Whelan warned FDA of serious health damage

In December 2020, Dr. J. Patrick Whelan of UCLA warned the U.S. FDA that the "viral spike protein that is the target of the important Covid vaccines is also one of the major substances causing damage to more distant organs, possibly including the heart, lungs and kidneys.

Dr. Whelan explained that it is not the virus, but the spike protein that is responsible for some people having such a difficult time recovering from Covid-19, and often continuing to have long-term health problems, including heart problems.

This is because the spike protein binds to ACE-2 receptors in the heart, and also in the brain and other organs such as the liver and kidneys. This can damage even the smallest blood vessels.

Whelan has therefore made it clear to the FDA that the spike protein "in" the vaccines causes serious health problems.

Pathologists and dentists also point to spike protein as a culprit

Dr. Richard Vander Heide, professor of pathology at Louisiana State University, performed autopsies on Covid-19 deaths and came to the same conclusion: the blood clots, which some of the deceased are full of, are caused by the spike protein.

Overweight people are especially at risk, as they often suffer from chronic inflammation.

Even dentists are sounding the alarm. They see previously healthy patients now getting gum inflammation, and think the spike protein is the culprit.

Pfizer is even experimenting on children, toddlers and babies

A 40-year-old California pregnancy medicine physician described the first dose of the Pfizer vaccine in a patient as "killing the fetus," causing the woman to miscarry six days later.

Meanwhile, vaccine manufacturer Pfizer continues to demonstrate that it no longer has any ethical boundaries.

Even children are now being used as guinea pigs for their experimental gene therapy 'vaccines'. A two-year-old toddler has already died from it.

Known for years that mRNA can be inhaled

It has been known for years that mRNA can be exhaled and inhaled, and in this way can serve as a passive vaccine. 'Does this mean that the Covid spike protein, which is produced by the human body after it has been vaccinated, can escape through the breath and infect unvaccinated people?' wonders Dr Mark Sircus, professor of natural oncology.

'It's a terrible thought that the lunatics who created the virus with 'gain of function' experiments are going hand in hand with similar lunatics in the pharmaceutical industry who are using their vaccine to spread spike proteins even more widely throughout the human population.'

A government that has your health at heart would stop vaccinating immediately

It seems obvious to me that any government that actually has the health of the people at heart would declare a moratorium on all Covid vaccinations right now, at least until more research has been done worldwide, before these vaccines indeed end in a deadly slaughter the likes of which the world has never seen before.

However, the opposite is true. The European government is working on a series of (constitutional) amendments that should make the taking away of our freedom and right of self-determination permanent, as well as pave the way for mandatory vaccinations.

Should it indeed come to this, then we can probably only conclude that our own government has declared itself the greatest enemy of public health, and is knowingly helping to carry out a potential genocide. We can only hope that there are enough politicians and parliamentarians in Brussels who will (again) listen to their conscience. A number of policy makers seem to have definitively lost their ability to do so.

Chapter 5: Protest = Terrorism?

No one wants to hear it, no one is allowed to say it, but everyone knows where this could end up.

While Europe steams full steam ahead toward implementing official discrimination by dividing society into the "good" (tested/vaccinated) and "bad" (untested/unvaccinated) people, the first ball is being thrown in the U.S. for what the ultimate goal of things like vaccine passports is: the complete removal of the "bad" people from society. The well-known journal Nature has published a call for the UN and all governments to take rock-hard measures to stop 'anti-vax aggression'. Here is how you, as an unvaccinated person, will soon be seen and treated: as a terrorist.

The fascism of murderous maniacs like Hitler and Stalin is making a full return. The Texan pediatrician Peter Hotez has become such an extreme corona idol that he puts people who are critical of vaccinations on a par with cyber criminals and nuclear terrorism. Using outright war language, he calls for a "counteroffensive" by governments to attack and silence anyone who opposes vaccinations.

'Counteroffensive against new destructive forces'

'Stopping the spread of the coronavirus requires a high-level counteroffensive against new destructive forces,' Hotez writes. 'Efforts must extend to the areas of cyber security, law enforcement, public education and international relations. A high-level inter-agency task force reporting to the UN secretary general could take stock of the overall impact of anti-vaccine aggression, and propose tough, balanced measures.'

'This task force should include experts who have tackled complex global threats such as terrorism, cyber attacks and nuclear armament. Indeed, anti-science is now approaching a similar level of threat. It is becoming increasingly clear that a counteroffensive is needed to promote vaccinations.'

Police and military against vaccine opponents

Hotez talks about "targeted attacks on scientists" allegedly committed by anti-vaxxers, but does not cite a single concrete example. To stop this fictitious "aggression," he literally advocates targeted (armed) attacks on anti-vaxxers. In fact, he wants the government to use the police and the army to deal with vaccine critics and refusers - in reality people who refuse to take part in these gene-manipulating experiments, which, according to official EU statistics, have already made enormous numbers of victims.

By placing this outrageous call, Nature, which was already completely in the pocket of the international vaccine mafia, which is now carrying out a monstrous genocidal experiment on the whole of humanity with the help of almost all governments, has lost its credibility once and for all.

Coarse violence against the 'wrong' people is considered okay again

Coarse violence against innocent men, women and children is evidently considered okay again. We have been warning for years against the return and even surpassing of the 1930s and 1940s, and now it is happening. If this isn't stopped, if people don't rise up en masse against this potential worst crime against humanity ever, it's going to end irrevocably as it did in the 1940s, namely with "facilities" where the unwanted "wrong" people are locked up and put away so that the rest of society can conduct itself "safely" again.

Or in other words: with concentration camps.

As long as people continue to deny that a repeat of this horrible history is possible, as long as people refuse to face the chilling parallels with Nazi Germany, the globalist forces of vaccination can continue unimpeded.

'The Russians' have done it again

And 'of course' also according to Hotez 'the Russians' are behind all the 'vaccine disinformation'. Then we forget for a moment that Russia was one of the first to develop a vaccine and begin administering it to its population.

No matter, because since last year the Western media have also definitively thrown off their last shred of feigned independence and objectivity, and are even proud to function as the propaganda organs of the Western establishment and the globalist climate-vaccine cult. By the way, we have been writing for years that "the Russians" will be blamed for just about everything, and that has the purpose of getting you to agree to - even call for - the planned Third World War against Russia, and most likely against China as well.

Humanity ruled by unscrupulous monsters

Unscrupulous monsters are at the helm of humanity, which, through blind obedience and unconditional docility, is itself being turned step by step into an equally unscrupulous monster. It is not yet too late, but there is very little time left to stop mandatory testing and vaccination passports, followed by mandatory testing and vaccinations, and then the imprisonment and eventual removal of the "wrong" unvaccinated - in Hotez' eyes the new "terrorists".

Chapter 6: Immune system suppression

Covid-19 is "mainly a vascular illness," according to researchers - Circulation Research: Lung injury is aided by spike protein - Your immune system is working against you to protect you from the vaccine.

In a scientific publication, researchers at the famed Salk Institute, which was founded by vaccine pioneer Jonas Salk, indirectly admit that the Covid vaccinations induce life-threatening blood clots and harm to both blood vessels and the immune system.

We noted earlier this week that an increasing number of well-known scientists are coming to the opinion that vaccines are the greatest hazard to human health.

Thousands of Europeans and Americans have already paid with their lives, and hundreds of thousands with their health, for their "voluntary" participation in history's greatest "medical" experiment.

In the West, all Covid vaccinations program the human body to create the spike protein, the most lethal element of the alleged SARS-CoV-2 virus, with the goal of shielding humans against the spike protein's damaging consequences.

In a nutshell, we make your body manufacture something harmful in order for it to generate antibodies against that same danger, but we have no idea how or if this process will ever be stopped.

So why not take the "risk" of getting the virus, which has been shown to not make 99.7% of the population sick, if at all? No, in 2021, that rational, historically uncontroversial line of reasoning is suddenly so antiquated. We can no longer rely on our natural immune system and must instead rely on what is administered through a syringe.

'Covid-19 is mostly a vascular illness,' says the researcher.

The vaccination industry, politicians, and the media continue to insist that the spike protein is safe, but the Salk Institute has now established that this is not the case. On the contrary, the Salk researchers and other scientific colleagues warn in the publication "The spike protein of the new coronavirus plays an extra crucial role in disease" that the spike protein harms cells, "confirming that Covid-19 is largely a vascular illness."

Another spike protein that has claimed so many lives?

Of course, the Salk scientists are forbidden from criticizing vaccines directly. That is why, according to their article, the spike protein produced by vaccines behaves quite differently than the spike protein produced by the alleged virus.

To begin with, this contradicts all vaccine makers' claims that their vaccines create the same spike protein. Second, it casts doubt on the efficacy of vaccines, because if the spike protein produced by vaccines differs significantly from that produced by the virus, what is the point of vaccination (assuming, for the time being, that these genetically designed 'vaccines' operate at all)?

On the plus side, even pro-vaccine scientists now accept that the spike protein is to blame for a large number of deaths and people suffering from major side effects and long-term, often permanent health harm. In other words, it's an implied admission that Covid-19 vaccinations are potentially fatal.

Spike protein causes lung injury, according to research published in Circulation Research.

"The SARS-Cov-2 spike protein impairs endothelial function by inhibiting ACE-2," according to a scientific study published in Circulation Research. The inside of the heart and blood vessels are lined with edothele cells. By decreasing ACE-2 receptors, the spike protein 'promotes lung injury.' The endothelial cells in blood arteries are damaged, and the metabolism is disrupted as a result.

The authors of this study were also pro-vaccination, claiming that "vaccine-generated antibodies" may protect the body from the spike protein. Essentially, the spike protein can cause significant damage to vascular cells, and the immune system can counteract this damage by fighting the spike protein.

The immune system is trying to protect you AGAINST the vaccine

In other words, the human immune system strives to defend the patient from the vaccine's negative effects and counter-reactions in order to prevent the patient from dying. Anyone who survives the Covid vaccine owes it to their own immune system's protection AGAINST the vaccine, not the vaccination itself.

'The vaccination is the weapon,' Mike 'Natural News' Adams concludes. 'Your immune system protects you. All Covid vaccinations should be withdrawn off the market immediately and re-evaluated for long-term negative effects based on this research alone.'

According to official VAERS statistics, the number of vaccine-related deaths in the United States in 2021 will be almost 4000 percent more than the total number of vaccine-related deaths in 2020.

The holy vaccine is not to blame for a heart attack or a cerebral hemorrhage.

The following mechanism has been scientifically proved and is now established: the Covid-19 vaccinations encourage your body to make the spike protein, which can cause vascular damage and blood clots, which can move throughout the body and end up in various organs (heart, lungs, brain, etc.). People who die as a result of this are referred to as having had a "heart attack," "blood clot," or "brain haemorrhage" - the sacrosanct vaccines can and must never be blamed, no matter how much evidence there is today showing they are the main reasons.

Vaccine recipients appear to offer a risk to the unvaccinated, in addition to the possibility for permanent or deadly harm to their own health. Many of the corona'wappies' who have recently had their shots have been transformed into walking'spike factories,' and can now exhale these spike proteins. They can so infect others through this 'shedding' process.

Bioweapon vaccines were created by the apartheid administration against the black population.

Vaccines have long been used as bioweapons against the general public. South Africa's Apartheid Government created the technology underlying such a "self-replicating" vaccination. Scientists were developing 'racial' vaccines at the time, with the goal of eradicating much of the black population.

This year, the Johns Hopkins Bloomberg School of Public Health proposed using a self-replicating vaccine to automatically 'vaccinate' the whole world's population.

Drones and AI robots would subsequently be used to enforce and monitor the program.

People who are still eager to sign up in a vaccine alley to be genetically modified to generate a potentially life-threatening spike protein appear to have been fully misled by the mainstream media and system politicians. They've been numb to all the warnings and the mountains of proof, and they can't believe the world is being ruled by unscrupulous monsters who have no qualms about committing the potentially single biggest genocide in human history.

Chapter 7: Passports & chips

A 2016 interview with WEF senior executive Klaus Schwab, in which he predicts that "within 10 years" an obligatory global health card will be adopted, and everyone will have implanted microchips, adds to the proof that the Covid-19 issue was painstakingly prepared.

Schwab was reportedly working on a plan at least five years ago to create a huge virus outbreak and exploit it to establish health passports and link them to mandatory testing and vaccinations, all according to the problem-reaction-solution approach. The goal is to have complete control over the whole human population on the planet.

'Within 10 years, we will have implanted microchips,' said Schwab five years ago.

In 2016, a French-speaking interviewer asked him, 'Are we talking about implantable chips?' 'When is it going to happen?'

'Absolutely in the next ten years,' said Schwab. 'We'll start by putting them in our clothes.' We can next picture implanting them in our brains or skin.' The WEF foreman then commented on his vision of man and machine 'fusing.'

'In the future, we may be able to communicate directly between our brains and the digital world.' We observe a merger of the physical, digital, and biological worlds.' People will simply have to think about someone in the future to be able to reach them straight through the 'cloud.'

There will be no more biological persons with natural DNA in the transhumanist world, which will finally become fully "digital." The 'cloud' will be used to store everyone's data.

Humanity has begun to be reprogrammed genetically.

The current economic order will be destroyed by Schwab's 'Great Reset' ('Build Back Better'). The looming financial meltdown will be exploited to launch a new global system based only on digital money and transactions. This new system will be connected to the entire world thanks to 5G technology. Refusers will be barred from "buying and selling," in other words, from social life.

In the late 2020s, Covid-19 mRNA 'vaccines' began genetically programming and manipulating humanity in order to make it 'fit' to be first linked, then integrated, with this global digital system, which, as you know, I believe is the Biblical realm of 'the Beast.'

These gene-altering vaccines have the potential to eliminate your free will and ability to think for yourself, as well as your desire and ability to connect with the spiritual realm.

Christian Perspective: Humanity is cut off from God

From a Christian perspective, the reprogramming of human DNA through these vaccines can be seen as Satan's final attempt to permanently separate humankind from God. This appears to be the true explanation for the prophetic Bible book of Revelation's warning that individuals who bear this "mark" will perish.

This isn't simply because of a chip and a succession of pricks; it's because of what those pricks will do to and in you. As a result, God will be unable to save those whose minds (free will) have been reprogrammed to total obedience ('worship'). That will necessitate His intervention, for otherwise, humanity as a whole will be lost forever.

False teachings have blinded a large portion of Christianity.

The essential aspect of this devious plot, which has been in the works for a long time, was the infiltration of Christianity with a series of false teachings, with the goal of keeping believers blind until the end of time in preparation for the advent and establishment of the Beast's rule.

Indeed, tens to hundreds of millions of Christians, particularly in the West, believe that they will never have to live through this period. Even now, when the implementation of this system has begun, the majority of people refuse to accept it. With their pro-vaccination views, most Christian parties and churches are openly cooperating in this "Great Reset" to the domain of "the Beast." In theological terms, the Vatican is the most powerful and convinced driver of this.

'But we were duped!' isn't an excuse.

Perhaps a biblical parallel can help some people understand? Genesis 3, the tale of creation and the 'Fall,' as told to us today: The serpent persuaded Adam and Eve that they were not allowed to 'eat' the 'apple,' in this case the sign, i.e. not to have it pricked in them (root test of 'the sign': charagma = scratch/something with a needle = prick), but the serpent persuaded them that this sign would not damn them, but rather make them into 'gods.' After being persuaded by this falsehood, their complaints against God ('but we've been lied to!') were futile, and they died slowly and painfully. They could have and should have known, thus they had no justification.

Accepting 'the sign,' according to the Bible, carries an even worse consequence: eternal death. Allowing yourself to be genetically modified with mRNA vaccinations and then integrated into a global digital network, so relinquishing all control over your body and free will, will be up to each individual to decide whether the danger is worth it.

Chapter 8: No more freedom

The US federal Occupational Safety and Health Administration (OSHA) is warning employers that they will be held liable for any damage to their employees' health if they are required to be vaccinated against Covid-19. This could become a tricky issue in Europe as well, since the government has rejected all government liability in advance and put it on the plate of health care providers. If in the end no agency wants to take responsibility, then in view of human rights these vaccinations cannot possibly be directly or indirectly made a condition for getting or having a job, or access to buildings and events, as is now the intention.

If a U.S. worker is forced to be injected with these experimental mRNA gene therapies packaged as "vaccines" and is subsequently blinded or paralyzed, or even dies, this injury will be considered "work related," which will make his employer liable. The guidelines also state that employers are required to record (serious) side effects and adverse reactions following Covid vaccinations in their employees.

The new OSHA directive was published on April 20, and was a response to companies and institutions that had announced that all their employees will be required to be vaccinated, such as the Methodist Hospital network in Houston. Those who refuse will first be suspended, and later fired.

Vaccines only have emergency authorization

It is expected that this hospital organization and many other employers will be sued if they follow through with these plans and their employees subsequently become ill or die. According to the VAERS registration system, nearly 200,000 Americans have already suffered health damage from the Covid-19 vaccines, and nearly 4,000 have died. Nearly 20,000 have been seriously (long-term or permanent) injured (autoimmune diseases, paralysis, blindness, the muscle disease ALS, Creutzfeld-Jakob, Alzheimer's, etc.).

America's Frontline Doctors (AFLDS) warns that the vaccines - as in Europe - have only a temporary emergency license, and for that reason alone cannot be imposed on anyone. 'The US Food & Drug Administration's emergency authorization specifically states that individuals should have the free choice to accept or refuse these vaccines,' LifeSiteNews explained. 'Many point out that any dismissal for refusing vaccines absolutely undermines your necessary freedom.'

However, the European Human Rights Court recently ruled that mandatory vaccinations are legal. Still, even in the Netherlands, not one worker should automatically accept that his boss requires a Covid-19 vaccination as a condition for keeping your job, or continuing to do the work for which you were hired.

Chapter 9: No healthcare

Some doctors are so indoctrinated and terrified that they blame the sick themselves: 'My employer put a lot of pressure on me to be vaccinated.'

The Highwire, the fastest growing American Internet health program that already has more than 75 million viewers, recently focused attention on a troubling trend in the U.S. that may also be occurring in other Western countries. In fact, more and more doctors are refusing to treat people who suffer from serious side effects and adverse reactions after vaccination with a Covid-19 vaccine. The reason is obvious: the political and pharmaceutical establishment has effectively canonized these gene-manipulated vaccines. If people do get very sick or even die from them - in the U.S. in 2021 there will already be 4000% more vaccine victims than in the whole of 2020 from all other vaccinations combined - then the instructions are that it cannot and must not be the vaccine's fault. Doctors who nevertheless observe this must fear for their jobs and careers.

Some doctors are so indoctrinated that they blame the sick themselves. They call people who suffer serious side effects after vaccination patients with a 'conversion disorder', afraid to put in their file that the vaccine is the probable cause. (Or, in other words, 'go back home, little lady, because it's between your ears.')

'On January 4, I was put under great pressure by my employer to get vaccinated,' Shawn Skelton told me. After she complied, she immediately experienced side effects such as mild flu-like symptoms. 'But by the end of the day, my legs were hurting so badly that I couldn't take it anymore. When I woke up the next day my tongue was twitching, and then it got worse and worse. The next day I had convulsions all over my body. That lasted 13 days.'

'Too afraid to treat us,' they say.

'One doctor told me the diagnosis was, 'I don't know what's wrong with you, therefore we blame you,'" said another. Skelton elaborated. 'Doctors just do not know how to address the mRNA vaccine's negative effects. I also believe they are terrified of it. I'm at a loss for words as to why no doctor wants to help us.'

Two other healthcare workers, Angelia Desselle and Kristi Simmonds had similar experiences. They too suffered convulsions, and their doctors also refused to treat them. A neurologist rejected Desselle's email referral to him. 'He was a movement disorder specialist, which I thought I needed. My primary care physician said it looked like I had advanced Parkinson's. But he emailed back that he had very complex duties, and he couldn't see me at that time.'

As other doctors likewise kept the door closed to her, she went to a neurologist without mentioning that she

had been vaccinated against Covid-19. 'I didn't want to be sent away again. But it is in my medical record, so when he looked at that he said 'so you took the vaccine?' And I said 'yes, but I didn't want to give you that information because I need help.' Now she is finally receiving treatment for her migraine attacks.
In Europe, general practitioners and specialists are subject to stringent regulations.

We don't know if general practitioners in Europe also refuse to treat vaccinated patients who become unwell. They are, however, prohibited from prescribing proven-effective and safe drugs to (suspected) corona patients, such as hydroxychloroquine and Ivermectin. Nothing should threaten the "holy" mass vaccination program - recovery: genetic engineering program, after all.

In Europe, general practitioners and specialists are subject to stringent regulations.

We don't know if general practitioners in Europe also refuse to treat vaccinated patients who become unwell. They are, however, prohibited from prescribing proven-effective and safe drugs to (suspected) corona patients, such as hydroxychloroquine and Ivermectin. Nothing should threaten the "holy" mass vaccination program - recovery: genetic engineering program, after all.

Earlier this year, the government put any responsibility for the consequences of the Covid vaccinations on the shoulders of health care providers and the people who are vaccinated with them. It is therefore not inconceivable that healthcare professionals and specialists in Europe will be reluctant to recognize, let alone treat, vaccination victims as such.

Chapter 10: Dare to speak

Vaccinating during a pandemic was previously considered "unthinkable" in science - until last year. An investigation has been begun on the growing risks of infection and death among vaccinated people.

Global mass vaccines against Covid-19 are "unthinkable," "unacceptable," and a "historic error," according to Luc Montagnier, a French virologist who won the Nobel Prize in 2008 for discovering HIV. Vaccinations are what cause 'variants,' and individuals die from the sickness as a result of them.

'Isn't this a tremendous oversight? It was both a scientific and a medical error. Montagnier remarked in a translated interview published last Tuesday by the RAIR Foundation USA, "It is an awful mistake." 'This will be documented in history books because the mutations are caused by vaccination.'

Many epidemiologists are aware of this, yet they remain silent about it, even when it comes to well-known issues like 'antibody-dependent enhancement': 'It is the virus's antibodies that allow the illness to worsen,' Montagnier stated earlier this month in an interview with Pierre Barnérias of Hold-Up Media.

Although variants (mutations) do develop naturally (but virtually always become less lethal and thus less hazardous), Covid vaccinations are now the primary drivers of this process. 'What is the virus's function? Is it going to die or will it find another way? The novel variations are clearly formed as a result of the intervention of certain antibodies.'

Vaccinating during pandemics was considered 'unthinkable' in science until last year.

Vaccinating during a pandemic was formerly considered "unthinkable" in science because it has been proven to increase the amount of sick individuals and deaths. Vaccinations have produced and resulted in the new variations. That is something you see in every country; it is the same everywhere. Vaccinations cause mortality in every country.'

Data from the University of Washington's Institute for Health Metrics and Evaluation was used in a video to highlight how the number of deaths rises substantially in all countries where immunizations have been implemented. Montagnier cited official WHO data showing that since the immunizations were started in January, not just the number of deaths, but also the number of new infections and sick persons has increased dramatically, "particularly among young people."

Infections and mortality after vaccines are being studied.

Thrombosis (blood clots) is one of the reasons why numerous countries have ceased using the AstraZeneca vaccine, according to the Nobel winner. He's also working on a study on people who get ill with the coronavirus after getting vaccinated. According to the CDC, at least 5,800 Americans had been affected by the virus by April; 396 of them were hospitalized, and 74 died.

"I will demonstrate that they are developing vaccine-resistant variations." Montagnier made headlines in April 2020 when he said that the SARS-CoV-2 virus had to have been created in a lab. 'The presence of HIV elements and malaria germs in the coronavirus genome is particularly suspicious.' These characteristics of the virus could not have developed spontaneously.' In July 2020, he published a study that backed up his idea.

Is there a mass euthanasia scheme in the works?

The argument that the Covid-19 vaccinations are more akin to a slow-motion euthanasia program, which could result in open genocide on an unprecedented scale in the short to medium term, looks increasingly justified. People who have recently been vaccinated and claim that "nothing bothers them" forget that (severe) vaccination harm might take weeks, months, or even years to manifest.

Because the virus has yet to be isolated anywhere in the globe, some believe the 'new coronavirus' is just a massive scam designed to inject people with this experimental gene therapy. As a result, the foundations are being laid for a transhuman RNA-DNA programming platform that might permanently alter, control, or cripple anyone who has received these vaccines.

Chapter 11: Poison mandate

'Poisoning risk from lethal phosgene gas'

The ingredients of the Moderna Covid-19 'vaccine' have been released by the Connecticut Department of Health. According to the package insert, this vaccine contains 'SM-102,' which is 'not acceptable for human or animal usage,' according to the manufacturer. The producer, Cayman Chemical Company, has told OSHA that this chemical produces 'acute poisoning' and is 'fatal on contact with the skin.' With prolonged or repeated exposure, SM-102 "damages the central nervous system, kidneys, liver, and respiratory system."

In brief, persons who receive this vaccine may become poisoned. Despite this, government and media efforts continue to tout the vaccinations' safety.

The Connecticut Department of Health's complete list of ingredients can be accessed online (archive here) (Natural News mirror Pre-vaccination screening form - V20, and Covid-19 vaccine ingredients list and spike protein schedule).

The government's guidelines to health-care facilities further state that the risk of anaphylactic shock from vaccinations is so high that all vaccination sites should have severe adverse response drugs on hand. Loss of consciousness, disorientation, confusion, weakness, diarrhea, nausea, vomiting, tunnel vision, seeing flashes of light, hearing issues, and hearing loss are among the many reported side effects. (And this for a virus that is completely harmless to 99.7% of the population.)

SM-102

After publishing this information, Hal Turner got numerous emails from people claiming that the SM-102 cautions only apply to chloroform, not Moderna's Covid vaccination. SM-102 is the third most prevalent element on the Moderna 'vaccine' ingredients list, and it IS the component, according to Cayman Chemical Company.'

'Deadly phosgene gas poisoning'

'Chloroform, like any other chemical, degrades. When it comes into contact with oxygen, it decomposes into phosgene gas,' which is a 'very poisonous gas (a mix of carbon monoxide and chlorine) that liquefies at +8 degrees,' according to the Van Dale Large Dictionary. At just 7 parts per million, it is fatal (7 parts per million).

'As a result, everyone who gets this shot could acquire chloroform, which can then decompose into phosgene gas as it circulates through their bodies.' Some, perhaps many, persons may achieve a deadly phosgene gas threshold in their body and die as a result, possibly within 180 days following their second dose.'

Phosgene poisoning can potentially lead to the formation of a pulmonary embolism. The patient's lungs fill with fluid, making it impossible for him or her to breathe - exactly what occurred to serious Covid-19 sufferers last year, placing them in the hospital and requiring life support.

'What an ingenious technique to depopulate the world - no one notices.'

'Once these people crash to the ground like flies, the same folks who gave us the vaccine may easily blame it on a Covid variation,' Turner concluded. 'How tragic that they died as a result of this mutation, which the vaccine failed to protect them from.' Could this be the case of mass murder's 'plausible deniability'? Make your own decision.' (Or it's being used to force yet another vaccine on the public.)

Turner concludes, 'What a fantastic method to depopulate the world.' 'No one notices because the deaths and the prick occur over a long period of time, and the symptoms of phosgene gas are identical to those of Covid.'

Turner's story was quickly labeled as "disinformation" by the Facebook "fact checker" Leadstories.com. Because these kinds of 'fact checkers' have been a major source of disinformation time and time again since last year, and appear to have been set up only to give the mainstream media's false propaganda a 'approval stamp,' this almost automatically means that there may be a large core of truth in it in 2021.

Leaflet with no content

A nurse had previously given Turner images of the obligatory package insert that will be included in the Moderna vaccination cartons. 'When I saw this, I was horrified,' the healthcare professional said. 'Can you tell me where the ingredients list is?' In fact, it turned out to be absolutely blank. 'There's nothing I've ever shot into a patient that looks like that.' They are aware of the contents.'

When it comes to information leaflets, do you know of a single vaccinated individual who received or downloaded and read one prior to 'the jab'? Foodstuffs must contain a long list of ingredients or they will not be sold. The same may be said for most common medicines and consumer goods. So why, of all things, is there an exception for vaccines? Why is it made as difficult as possible for you to learn what you're injecting into your body and the potential consequences?

Would you buy soup with the label "We'll know if the ingredients are safe in three years"?

Would vaccination proponents still refuse to consider it if they read the horrific package insert for the AstraZeneca/Vaxzevria vaccine, which reads: "Contains a chimpanzee-derived genetically modified adenovirus produced in human embryonic kidney cells." GVOs (genetically modified organisms) are present in this product.' ('A single dose (0.5 ml) comprises at least 250 million infectious units of chimpanzee adenovirus, which encodes the SARS-CoV-2 spike glycoprotein ChAdOx1-S.')

What about the black-and-white reality that the vaccine's efficacy, stability, and safety do not have to be shown clearly until May 31, 2022? That is not until March 31, 2024, or THREE YEARS from now, for the old and chronically ill (pg.16). What would vaccination supporters do if they went to the grocery to buy a can of soup and saw on the label that it wouldn't be known whether the components in that soup were safe for their health for another year or three? Wouldn't they then decide, "We're not going to do it for a bit, we'll take something else?"

Chapter 12: Toxic blood

For the time being, the Red Cross in Japan and Belgium do not accept blood donations from anyone who have been vaccinated against Covid-19. According to Jeffrey Kingston, head of Asia studies at Temple University, Japan has not forgotten the crisis in the 1980s, when the government approved the use of HIV-infected donor blood. This happened despite the fact that it was already known that heating might kill virus particles in the blood.

Only 2% of Japanese people are still fully vaccinated - recovery: gene manipulation therapy, compared to 35% in the United States. The Japanese government, according to Kingston, is not only bureaucratic, but also cautious. There is a typical waiting period for blood donation after other immunizations. This is 24 hours for influenza, cholera, and tetanus, 2 weeks for hepatitis B, and 4 weeks for measles, mumps, and rubella.

For the time being, the Belgian Red Cross does not accept donations from those who have been vaccinated.

The American Red Cross enables people who have had mRNA corona vaccines to donate blood in the same way that persons who have been infected with the coronavirus are allowed to. We couldn't discover anything concerning blood donations on the Red Cross website, so we think they can continue without limitation.

To date, no respiratory virus has been proved to be transmissible through blood, including coronaviruses and the flu virus. As a result, giving and receiving blood is risk-free,' according to the Belgian Red Cross website.

'However, unlike the usual flu vaccine, you will be momentarily unable to give after having a corona vaccination.' The length of time depends on the brand and whether you have symptoms after receiving the vaccine.' (Italics added) What are the signs and symptoms of? Surely, if you've been vaccinated, you're safe? Aren't these immunizations "proved safe"?

Chapter 13: India is crumbling

Millions of Indians wash in the Ganges River's open sewers, where dozens of bodies are now discovered everyday.

The number of deaths due to Covid-19 each day has risen from less than 100 in January to over 4,500 in May since India began its vaccine campaign. The clear link between immunizations and autism is no longer debatable. Also keep in mind RIVM director Jaap van Dissel's warning from late last year, when he anticipated that immunizations "could initially raise mortality." And that is exactly what is happening in many nations, including India on a massive scale.

Hundreds of dead are discovered in the Ganges every day. Thousands of Indians die every day from illnesses such as tuberculosis, typhoid, malaria, cholera, and influenza as a result of the country's still-poor sanitary and nutritional circumstances.

People who would have received Covid-19 appear to be more susceptible to the once-rare fungal infections mucormycosis and scrub typhus, which prey on the immune system's weakness. Scrub typhus affects about 1 million Asians each year, but the main threat is (drug-resistant) tuberculosis, which affects 2.8 million Indians each year and kills 435,000.

The death toll skyrockets after immunizations begin, going from fewer than 100 per day to over 4500 per day.

Over 186 million Indians have been immunized with the Covid-19 vaccine since January. India was doing quite well before the vaccine campaign began. The average number of deaths linked to Covid increased from well under 100 in the first three months of the global lockdowns to approximately 1000 in September and October 2020, before decreasing back to far under 100 in January.

Then immunizations were implemented, and the death toll skyrocketed to 1500 per day in April and nearly 4500 in May. In fact, 3532 Covid variants are currently circulating in India, all of which appeared nearly immediately after vaccines began.

How is this possible when two-thirds of the population has already developed antibodies, according to a private testing company? In April, the journal Nature asked the same question. Why are 45 times as many people suddenly dying today, if the immunizations were already protecting so many people against Covid-19? Could this be due to Antibody Dependent Enhancement (ADE), which has been warned about by a number of scientists and experts, and which could become a problem in the Netherlands in the fall when the corona and other respiratory viruses return?

'People who have been vaccinated are more susceptible to major illnesses and infections.'

'Not only do vaccines poison people's systems, making them more susceptible to infectious consequences (virus interference), but they also lead the immune system to fail if it is re-exposed to 'live' coronavirus mutations (ADE),' says Mike 'Natural Adams.'

According to Adams, clinical research have indicated that the Covid-19 vaccinations made recipients more vulnerable to more severe illnesses. The large number of patients who have experienced adverse effects from these vaccines, including as tiredness, fever, harvesting problems, lethargy, paralysis, blood clots, and so on, is proof that they induce significant illnesses, further weakening the immune system.

'Bioweapons of autoimmunity'

'A widespread vaccination program could encourage coronaviruses to evolve even quicker, resulting in increased Spike protein change and, as a result, the creation of novel varieties. The B.1.617.2 variety spreading in India, according to British scientists, is 50 percent more contagious.' By the way, this is a common occurrence; changing viruses always get more contagious, but almost usually become less lethal. However, thanks to vaccines, this time could be different, as the bloodbath in India seem to imply.

Furthermore, these vaccinations act as autoimmune disease bioweapons, prompting people's bodies to manufacture Spike proteins, which can be released into the environment and lead to the rapid evolution of infectious virus particles. After that, the unvaccinated are exposed to a variety of Spike proteins from the vaccinated. This could explain why India's death toll has suddenly skyrocketed, and why bodies are washing up in droves along the Ganges' banks.'

Chapter 14: The next pandemic?

The World Economic Forum, like the World Health Organization, has emerged as one of the most vehement foes of liberty and humanity.

Planned (false flag) WEF cyber attack to destabilize financial system between August 2021 and March 2022 - Will the next "killing virus" be SARS-3, which has already been produced in an Italian laboratory, or SPARS?

The global power elite is so empowered by 90 percent of the population's slavish devotion and naive gullibility that no effort is made to hide the reality that one large planned and predetermined scenario is actually being enacted.

WHO Director Tedros Adhanom Ghebreyesus, a committed communist, is now openly proclaiming the next pandemic, which will be "more more contagious and lethal" than Covid-19, as you may know. Pharmaceutical companies are rubbing their palms together and have already started preparing and testing the next round of vaccinations.

'Make no mistake, this is not the last time the world faces a pandemic threat,' Tedros told the UN General Assembly of 194 member states' health ministers. 'It is an evolutionary certainty that another virus will emerge that is much more contagious and lethal than this one.'

'Evolutionary certainty' was a euphemism for 'this is what we, like Covid-19, have painstakingly developed and planned in collaboration with the World Economic Forum.' Maybe the other virus is SPARS, which we wrote about earlier this year and was supposed to arrive in (about) 2025? Will it be SARS-3, which has already been produced in an Italian facility and might be released on the general public at any time?

'The death toll is dropping, but we're not out of the woods yet.'

Of course, the WHO chief had to declare that the number of Covid-19 cases and deaths had been steadily declining for the past three weeks. To do otherwise would make it very clear that immunizations are having the exact opposite effect in places such as India. Since vaccines began, the number of daily deaths has climbed from 100 to nearly 4500 each day. The guidelines for the heavily overused PCR test were "secretly" modified in January, ostensibly to make the immunizations look successful.

Vaccines are now being evaluated.

Pharmaceutical companies, who have seen how profitable vaccinating during a pandemic can be during the last year, are already working on new vaccinations. Last Monday, Bloomberg reported that GlaxoSmithKline (together with partner Sanofi) is working on the next generation of Covid vaccinations. A trial session using a new vaccination on more than 37,000 patients will begin as early as next week, according to Roger Connor, chief of vaccine development.

It is necessary to bring the population to its knees.

It is now safe to say that the established globalist order, led by the World Economic Forum, the United Nations, the World Health Organization, the International Monetary Fund, the European Union, and the Gavi alliance, and backed by almost every political party, has launched a frontal assault on humanity. As you may be aware, Phase 2 of this pandemic has already been announced: a (false flag) cyber attack on the (bankrupt) Western financial system, as well as possibly the energy supply, with the goal of bringing the population to its knees and forcing them to accept the communist 'Great Reset' ('Build Back Better'), or the 'Fourth Industrial Revolution' in the framework of UN Agenda 21/2030, without resistance.

The WEF has been running simulations, similar to the corona pandemic simulation in October 2019 ('Event 201'), to see how best to carry out such a cyber-attack, which will cut the population off from their bank accounts, possibly the internet, and possibly even (parts of) their energy supply (and thus transportation and food supply) for days-perhaps weeks-and how to make the most of the expected consequences.

According to Armstrong, the recent cyber attack on the Colonial Pipeline in the United States, which was allegedly blocked by hackers and then released after paying a $5 million extortion fee, was also a test to see if the planned cyber attack on the financial system could be carried out in this manner. 'They can now argue that malware is profitable, and the entire globe is at risk.' That's the most likely scenario right now.'

'This threat appears to be motivated by the desire to complete the Great Reset.' Covid was grossly inflated, and those behind the bogus models that were used to flatten the global economy stand to make a lot from inflating this cyber danger. The question now is, when will they do it? 'Will it be this year or next year?'

Chapter 15: Total control?

The first components required to transform the entire human race into total techno-slaves are already being extensively distributed.

Radio waves and magnetic fields can be used to make brain and nerve cells sensitive - controlling human behavior in locations with particular radiation is becoming a reality.

Researchers in the United States have created a magnetic protein that can be used to stimulate brain cells quickly (and vice versa). This novel technique can be used to regulate the areas of the brain responsible for complicated behavior.

Because the development of the Spike protein is important to mRNA vaccinations against the coronavirus, it's easy to envisage that in the future, this sort of vaccine will include another "program" that develops a protein meant to obtain external control over our behavior and thoughts.

Optogenetics is being phased out in favor of chemogenetics.

Optogenetics is the most powerful approach. Laser light pulses can be used to switch on or off clusters of associated neurons. Chemogenetics is a new approach that has recently been created. This works by activating customized proteins with "designer pharmaceuticals" (drugs, vaccinations) that can be targeted to certain cell types.

The downside of optogenetics is that it necessitates the introduction of fiber optic wires into the brain, which can only penetrate the tissue to a limited amount. Chemogenetics uses biological reactions to activate nerve cells in a matter of seconds. It is no longer necessary to "open up" the brain with this new approach.

Project magneto

Previous research has shown that nerve cells' heat and mechanical pressure-activated proteins can be genetically changed to become responsive to radio waves and magnetic fields. Attaching a (para)magnetic particle to them, as well as short DNA sequences, accomplishes this. This method has already been utilized to control glucose levels in mice's blood.

In a lab experiment, the created 'Magneto' protein was found to be capable of being taken up by human kidney cells. The protein was then triggered using a magnetic field. 'Magneto' was then put into the genome of a virus, together with a green fluorescent protein and DNA sequences that exclusively target specific types of neurons, in a subsequent test. After that, the virus was delivered into the brains of mice. Magneto was activated there using a magnetic field, causing the (brain) cells to create particular nerve impulses.

Then it was the turn of the mice who could move about freely. Magneto was injected into the region of the brain that controls motivation and reward (dopamine neurons). The mice were then separated into groups and placed in a room where some were exposed to a magnetic field while others were not.

The Magneto mice were found to spend significantly more time in the magnetic area because dopamine neurons in their brains were engaged, giving them a sense of reward when they were there. This demonstrated that complicated behavior may be controlled and even directed by employing Magneto neurons located deep in the brain.

Steve Ramirez, a Harvard neurologist, is ecstatic about the new strategy. 'This method consists of a single, beautiful virus that can be injected anywhere in the brain,' says the researcher. To alter the behavior of the animals (and later humans?), they merely needed to be exposed to a magnetic field.

Controlling your behavior in a radiation-affected area is becoming more feasible.

Now that humans in the year 2021 are having genetic (mRNA) instructions injected into their systems under the pretext of "vaccines" to produce a protein (the

Spike protein), the next step is to add OTHER instructions to these types of vaccines. In a 2017 speech, Moderna's CMO outlined how mRNA can be used to edit people's DNA, making mRNA "vaccines" a platform via which humans can be programmed.

And it appears that this is exactly what will be done, with proteins that will change your behavior when you are in an area with certain radiation coming soon (such as 5G). Until it is a fait accompli, the mainstream media will no certainly call it a "conspiracy theory" or "disinformation." Protesting then becomes meaningless, as you will most likely not be able or willing to do so due to this new technology.

As a result, when WEF CEO Klaus Schwab declared last year that you will "own nothing and be happy" by 2030 (but maybe much sooner), he was dead serious. You will, in fact, be hardwired to be happy no matter what the circumstances are. Some people appear to be impatient to surrender their humanity, independent thought, and even their "soul" in order to become willless, programmed, controlled, and digitally managed system slaves.

Chapter 16: Mask the sheep

Scientists believe that face masks worn by the general public pose an infection risk - For over a century, all pandemic experiences have demonstrated that face masks do not work in fighting viruses and are ineffective as protection.

Recently, the mainstream media triumphantly released a study proving that mouthguards are effective. However, a brief look at the study's commissioner revealed all: the Max Planck Institute, which is substantially supported by the German government and the European Union. What is today considered'science' will almost certainly be 'whose bread you eat...' in 2020 and 2021.

As a result, we can no longer anticipate impartial or critical conclusions from these types of 'we of WC duck...' researchers; instead, they let themselves to be exploited, just as they were in the past, to stamp government programs with approbation. In fact, a recent comprehensive German meta-study concluded that mouthguards are not only ineffective but also hazardous to one's health.

After an hour of reading on the Max Planck Institute's website, it's evident that the institutes and scientists linked with them are like two hands in one glove when it comes to dealing with the government. There are no critical notes, and there isn't a single study that contradicts the authorities' claims even marginally. We also read a request to do more to combat anti-vaccine voices, such as banning them from the Internet, in order to make it more "democratic"...

The Inquisition has returned under another name

The politically powerful Catholic Church dragged Galileo Galilei before the Inquisition at the beginning of the 17th century because, like Copernicus in the 16th century, he claimed that the earth, like the other planets, revolves around the sun (the heliocentric worldview), and that we are not the center of the universe (the geocentric worldview). To 'prove' him wrong, several established'scientists' and'scientific' and theological theses were quoted. Only in 1992 did the then-Pope John Paul II apologize, and the Vatican cleansed his name.

Mouthguards are ineffective and (very) hazardous to one's health, according to a metastudy.

However, there are still those scientists who have not sold their souls to the devil. For example, a recent German meta-study confirmed what has been known for over a century: mouthguards are ineffective and harmful to one's health. Twenty-two of the 44 scientific research that found substantial detrimental effects of mouthguards were published in 2020, and twenty-two of those studies were published under Covid-19. There were 31 experimental studies and 13 observational studies in total. The well-known blue mouthguards and N95 mouthmasks drew 68 percent of the attention.

Exhaustion, confusion, and sickness are caused by increased respiratory difficulty, heart rate, and blood pressure.

Wearing surgical (blue) mouth caps by healthy healthcare workers (18 to 40 years old) causes measurable physical effects with increased transcutaneous (through the skin) CO_2 values and significant changes in blood composition after only 30 minutes, according to a randomized crossover study published in 2005. The considerable rise in CO_2 "breathing back in" causes increased respiratory resistance, requiring the body to exert increasing amounts of effort, as well as a large increase in heart rate.

The negative effects may appear minor at first, but wearing mouthguards on a regular basis adds up to an increasing physical load. Mouthguards are predicted to have disease-relevant impacts in the long run, according to the warning. High blood pressure, arteriosclerosis, heart disease (metabolic syndrome), and neurological diseases are just a few of the unavoidable side effects of long-term use of mouth masks.

Even a small increase in CO_2 in the inhaled air causes headaches, respiratory issues (asthma), elevated blood pressure and heart rate, which causes blood vessel damage, and finally neuropathological and cardiovascular disorders. Only slightly raised respiratory pressure over a long period of time has similar effect. Elevated CO_2 levels are especially dangerous for pregnant women because they impair the placenta's blood supply.

Panic attacks, hyperventilation, cognitive difficulties, and headaches are all symptoms of stress.

It has been established beyond a reasonable doubt that mouthguards cause significant and, in the long run, lasting health damage. The stress hormone norepinephrine is released very instantly by the human brain in response to low oxygen levels and slightly increased CO_2 consumption. The CO_2 level only needs to be 5% to produce a panic attack in 15 to 16 minutes, according to breath provocation experiments. The usual CO_2 concentration in exhaled air is around 4%.

Mouth caps are contraindicated for epileptics, according to neurologists from the United States, the United Kingdom, and Israel, since they can cause hyperventilation. In fact, wearing a mouthguard can raise your breathing rate by 15% to 20%.

The use of mouthpieces caused 71.4 percent of 343 health care employees in New York to experience recognized physical (illness) symptoms. Even worse, 28% had chronic health issues for which they needed medication.

Within the context of Covid-19, all varieties of mouthguards were evaluated in depth in 2020. Conclusion: After only 100 minutes, they create severe thinking and concentration issues, which are produced directly by the decreasing oxygen content in the blood. Another study discovered that mouthguards are directly responsible for more than half of the headaches experienced by mouthguard users.

Infections and skin conditions

Because mouth caps cover the respiratory tract, body temperature rises and humidity rises, drastically altering the skin's natural habitat. Many people have red, itchy, and dry skin, as well as excessive sebum production (acne). It worsens and prolongs skin disorders, making people more susceptible to infections. This is because both the blue and N95 mouthguards allow germs, fungus, and viruses to multiply fast both within and outside the mouthguards (which are saturated after only 10-15 minutes and then no longer operate anyhow).

The skin on your face is not meant to stay hidden for long periods of time. Large numbers of people will experience undesirable skin problems now that it is required to do so anyway.

Significant psychological harm, particularly among children

73

Psychological damage has been documented in addition to the numerous physical repercussions and substantially diminished quality of life - because even regular daily activities such as eating, drinking, and conversing are badly affected. Mouthguards cause a sensation of loss of freedom and autonomy (which may very well be the aim of the wearing requirement), which can lead to suppressed rage and unconscious continual distraction, especially since mouthguards are frequently imposed by others.

Mouthguards jeopardize basic human rights such as personal integrity, the right to self-determination, and autonomy, in addition to causing discomfort and resulting in the loss of certain psychomotor, cognitive, and mental abilities, as well as reduced reactivity. Mouthguards are especially damaging to children, who often experience worry and tension as a result of them. Many youngsters get unwell and unhappy, retreat, and engage less in life. (An entire generation of youngsters and teenagers has thus been severely harmed.)

The media, both now and in the past, has played a very harmful role.

Depressive feelings are widespread, with 50 percent of the oral health wearers polled experiencing them. The concern is exacerbated by the mainstream media's frequently exaggerated and one-sided reporting. Only 38% of media coverage of the Ebola pandemic in 2014 contained scientific fact, and 42% (significantly) overstated the danger, according to a research. A shocking 72 percent of media pieces were designed to make viewers feel worse about their health.

We don't have hard numbers yet, but we believe that by 2020, just 10% of news coverage will contain any scientific fact, and 90% will (seriously) hype the coronavirus's danger. And, with a few exceptions, all mainstream media were and are guilty of instilling feelings of fear and uncertainty 24 hours a day, 7 days a week.

Mouthguards are a symbol of pseudo-solidarity and conformity.'

According to scientists in one of the papers analyzed, mouthguards have become "a symbol of conformity and pseudo-solidarity." The WHO, for example, exclusively emphasizes the ostensible 'benefits' of wearing mouthguards and attempts to create in the wearers the (false) belief that they are helping to combat a virus.

Meta-study conclusion: 'The potentially drastic and undesirable effects observed in multidisciplinary fields underscore the general scope of global decisions to introduce mouthguards... According to the literature, there are unequivocal, scientifically substantiated undesirable consequences for mouthguard wearers, both physical, psychological and social.'

'There is no scientific evidence that the virus has been eradicated.'

'Neither the WHO, the ECDC (European Centre for Disease Prevention and Control), nor national institutes (such as the RIVM) have proven with well-founded scientific data a positive consequence of mouthguards for the population (in the sense of a reduced spread of Covid-19),' the harsh mouthguard judgment reads.

'National and international health authorities have imposed their theoretical judgements on mouthguards on society, contrary to the scientifically established standard of evidence-based medicine, even though the mandatory wearing of mouthguards creates a deceptive sense of security.'

'Mouthguards worn by the general public pose a risk of infection.'

'From an infectious epidemiology standpoint, regular usage of mouthguards exposes wearers to the danger of self-contamination from both the inside and outside (of the mouthguards), as well as through contaminated hands. Furthermore, exhaled air causes mouthguards to get saturated, allowing infection-causing chemicals to gather on the inside. This tendency may be evidenced by the remarkable surge in rhinoviruses in the RKI (German National Institute of Public Health and the Environment) Sentinel research starting in 2020.'

'Mouthguards worn by the public are considered an infection risk by scientists, since standardized hygiene rules in hospitals cannot be followed by society.' On top of that, the forced 'having to speak louder under a mouthguard leads to an increased production of aerosols (the atomization effect)' (which can be measured up to 20 meters away, and which automatically makes all the social distancing completely useless, since mouthguards are thus saturated after only 10 - 15 minutes and no longer work anyway. And who replaces his or her mouthguard every 10 minutes?).

Mouthguards do not aid in any modern epidemic.

Mouthguards in daily usage failed to accomplish the hoped-for results in the fight against viral infections during the influenza pandemics of 1918-1919, 1957-1958, 1968, 2002, and with SARS 2004-2005, as well as the influenza of 2009 (swine flu).

The experiences prompted scientific studies, which concluded in 2009 that daily usage of mouthguards has no substantial antiviral effect. Even later, scientists and institutes determined that the mouthguards were ineffective in protecting users from viral respiratory infections. Surgical mouthguards, even when used in hospitals, lack solid evidence of virus prevention.'

'As always, no favorable benefits on infections or diseases have been detected in a practical comparison between Sweden and Belarus on the one hand and the rest of Europe, as well as the United States (between the states with and without mandatory mouthguards).

Chapter 17: Vaccine victims

'Thousands of avoidable deaths due to Covid, and thousands already owing to vaccines' - India halts death explosion following Ivermectin and hydroxychloroquine vaccinations - Could it be the same here with the same immunizations if such procedures are used in America?

Professor Dr. Peter McCullough, one of the world's foremost authorities on the treatment of Covid-19, accused the US government of concealing "unimaginable numbers" of vaccine victims in an interview.

This is exactly the scenario we've been forecasting for almost a year: vaccines produce enormous numbers of new casualties, which are then attributed to a Covid variation or some other cause of death, as is most likely the case in, example, India. Could this be the case here as well, if such techniques are already being used in America to persuade as many people as possible to take these 'vaccines'?

We are now being controlled by the same power elite (WEF, UN/WHO, Gavi/Gates, Big Pharma).

With the VAERS vaccination registration system in the United States, the number of reported vaccination deaths is approaching 5000, up from roughly 1% to a maximum of 10% of the real number in the past. As of May 15, about 11,500 individuals have been injured in the EU, with over 630,000 individuals hurt on both sides of the Atlantic and tens of thousands more people permanently ill or incapacitated. Because the number of vaccine victims is thousands of times larger than all other vaccines combined, a detailed study is usually required.

A medication is normally taken off the market after 50 deaths.

'Any new drug with five unexplained deaths gets a 'black box' warning, and then you hear on the news that this drug can kill you,' McCullough explained. 'And after 50 deaths, it's removed off the market,' says the author.

During the 1976 swine flu pandemic, the US sought to vaccinate 55 million people, but the effort was halted after 25 people died and 500 people were crippled as a result of the vaccine.

Now the exact opposite is happening in both America and Europe: the further the number of victims rises, the more pressure the authorities exert on the population to be vaccinated. And all this with substances that have only been provisionally approved, and whose producers will only have to prove that they are 'safe' in a few years' time.

'It would be impossible for civil service doctors to certify that deaths were not caused by immunizations in such a short period of time.'

The numbers are even falsified on purpose, according to the esteemed academic. At the end of March, there had been 2,602 vaccine-related deaths in the United States. The FDA then said that 1600 deaths had been 'investigated' by anonymous government doctors, who had come to the conclusion that none of these persons had died as a result of the vaccine.

'That was disturbing,' McCullough said. He knows from his own experience that it normally takes months to complete such an investigation, not just a few days or weeks. 'I've been chairman and participated on dozens of safety monitoring boards ... and I can tell you that there is no way that unknown civil service doctors without any experience with Covid-19 can determine that not one of these deaths was due to the vaccine.'

Many more people are dying in actuality.

Because only 1% to 10% of vaccine deaths are reported historically, as validated by a Harvard study, many more people will die in actuality than are reported in official estimates, and certainly not 0.
Because only 1% to 10% of vaccine deaths are reported historically, as validated by a Harvard study, many more people will die in actuality than are reported in official estimates, and certainly not 0.

Compare it to the flu vaccination. Annually, the VAERS reports 20-30 deaths, out of 195 million vaccinations.

With Covid-19, the US was already at 2602 deaths at 77 million vaccinations, by far the highest number for vaccines in all of history. Despite this, not one established politician or journalist in the mass media is demanding an independent investigation. Worse, the few who do are immediately stigmatized and reviled.

'It is estimated that 85 percent of all lives lost could have been saved.'

The Covid expert thinks that the thousands of deaths (about 16000 in the EU and the US in mid-May, certainly at least 1000 to 2000 more by now) and hundreds of thousands of sick and wounded will continue indefinitely. Furthermore, he said before the United States Senate on November 19, 2020, that "we now believe that up to 85% of the lives lost may have been saved with a multi-drug regimen."

However, those proven working and safe drugs are strictly prohibited in America, Europe and the Netherlands to apply to (presumed) Covid-19 patients. general practitioners can be fined €150,000 if they prescribe Ivermectin.

The government is completely in the bag of Big Pharma and Bill Gates-controlled institutions such as the WHO, and has decided from the outset that only a vaccine may bring 'salvation'.

India uses Ivermectin and HCQ to put a stop to the mortality toll.

India has begun employing Ivermectin and hydroxychloroquine, much against the interests of the WHO and Big Pharma (HCQ). As a result, the enormous increase in the number of deaths following the introduction of vaccinations has now come to an end.

The mainstream media has been told not to publish any criticism of vaccines.

All mainstream media, on the other hand, has been told to portray these drugs in a negative light and to publish (almost) no critical reporting concerning vaccines. They even purposefully generate as much anxiety as possible in Europe at the government's request.

This blatant censorship and total media corruption falls under the Trusted News Initiative, in which not only the social media giants such as Facebook, Google/YouTube and Twitter but also the major news agencies AP, Reuters and AFP participate, as well as the BBC, CBC, EBU (European Broadcasting Union), Microsoft and the Washington Post. Facts about the dark side of experimental gene-therapy vaccinations should be called "dangerous disinformation" by the mainstream media.

Since it results in so many avoidable deaths, how can this be labeled anything other than medical fascism or even medical terrorism?

'If citizens were given 'any type of honest, balanced news on safety,' McCullough concluded, 'they simply would not take this vaccine.' 'The Trusted News Initiative is really concerning, because we are currently experiencing a record number of deaths, which is increasing daily.'

The government and Big Pharma have a symbiotic connection.

The renowned physician claimed that the government and Big Pharma have an incestuous relationship, which prohibits regulatory organizations such as the WHO from being able, willing, or able to deliver an objective judgement. The American National Institutes of Health, for example, is a co-owner of the Moderna patent. As a result, the government has a financial incentive to sell and administer as many vaccines as feasible.

The few doctors, scientists and other professionals who do listen to their conscience are usually too afraid to speak out by name. Understandably, because otherwise since last year it is not only immediately the end of license or end of career, but you are also dragged through the mud and in some cases even sued and / or intimidated by the same government.

'We never find out the true number of casualties.'

According to a recent assessment of 500 nursing home residents conducted by a Kansas City doctor, 22 elderly persons died within 48 hours of receiving a Pfizer shot. 'I can't prove that the vaccine killed them all, but I can show that it killed them all within 48 hours. They only have to be monitored for 15 minutes, according to the guidelines, so we never get to see the real numbers. It's tough to prove if it happens after those 15 minutes... May God help us if the FDA authorizes this.

One courageous Canadian physician did step into the open. Dr. Charles Hoffe broke with a government ban on him speaking, saying that 'the Moderna vaccine has killed and disabled patients.'

'The government has never been interested in treating sick people.'

According to McCullough, the government had little interest in treating sick people (with drugs), but instead quickly adopted the WHO agenda (social distancing only, mouthguards, lockdowns, testing, and waiting for vaccinations).

He describes a four-step strategy in his paper "A Guide for Home-Based Covid-19 Treatment: A Step-by-Step Doctor's Plan That Could Save Your Life" (December 2020), where the most important pillar, treating and curing Covid-19 patients with proven and safe medications, has been completely absent from public policy. He believes that as a result, tens of thousands of people have died needlessly in the United States alone.

Last year, French academic Christian Perronne, who has a long and illustrious career, wrote a book with the provocative title "Is There a Mistake They Didn't Make?" - Covid-19: The holy marriage of incompetence and hubris.' According to him, if corona patients had been treated with zinc, hydroxychloroquine/quercetin, vitamins C and D, and azithromycin from the start (especially as a preventive measure), there would have been few deaths and 25,000 French people (80 percent of the death toll at the time) would still be alive today.

Chapter 18: Humanity is shrinking

Earth is still incredibly barren: there are few indications of human civilisation visible from space. - 'In New York, all of the people on the planet will fit into one-story buildings.' - "Having children should actually be a societal duty," says a Tesla executive who is focused on human RNA and DNA programming.

Elon Musk, the CEO of Tesla, is notorious for making statements that contradict the globalist 'New World Order' image. In a recent address, he stated that our greatest challenge in 20 years will be underpopulation, not overpopulation. We previously said that, contrary to common assumption, the Earth has more than enough room, food, energy, and riches to support at least three times as many people in a prosperous existence. As soon as possible. The true source of our greatest concern is the global power elite, who are doing everything imaginable to eliminate as many people as possible by keeping them impoverished, sick, hungry, and therefore controllable.

'I want to emphasize that the biggest issue in 20 years is population collapse, not an explosion.' He gives as a simple example someone who randomly drops a bomb from an airplane somewhere on earth. 'How often do you hit someone then? As a matter of fact, never. All kinds of stuff falls to Earth from space all the time. Natural meteorites, old rocket parts, but nobody worries about that.'

'Having children should almost be regarded as a social obligation.'

'All of the people in the planet could fit on one floor in New York.' The other floors are unnecessary.' According to Musk, we are so thinly dispersed throughout the world that we are barely visible from space. 'We must be wary about population collapse.' A low birth rate is a major danger.' He cautions that as a result, our culture may perish. 'That would be a depressing conclusion.' The average age would be extremely high, and the young would be forced to care for the elderly like slaves.'

'I believe that, to some extent, people must begin to regard having children as a civic obligation... Otherwise, humanity will perish. Quite literally. Wealth, education, and religion are all inversely connected to the birth rate. The more devout a person is, the more children he or she has.' It will be "as if someone killed half the (future) population" in a few decades. Something needs to be turned around.'

'As quickly as feasible, we must abandon fossil fuels'

Musk is, of course, totally committed to the green'sustainability' mission as an e-car creator and producer. He is upbeat about this since he feels China is also leading the way in this area, having already produced half of the world's electric vehicles. He believes that the world should transition away from fossil fuels as soon as feasible and toward "sustainable" solar, wind, and water energy, as well as nuclear energy in some situations.

The Tesla front man says that oil, gas and coal are running out fast, but forgets that this has been shouted for almost 50 years, and new reserves are constantly being discovered that can provide humanity with cheap energy for at least another century, and probably even many centuries.

Why are there CO2 taxes?

He also contends that society is not being charged for the full price of fossil fuels and CO2 emissions. As a result, he advocates for hefty global CO2 taxes.

Here too he forgets something important, namely that on a geological time scale there is still extremely little CO_2 in the atmosphere (about 450 ppm), and that despite all human CO2 emissions (which is only a percentage of far behind the decimal point). Moreover, all the geological evidence shows that CO2 levels only rise after temperatures rise, and not the other way around, as has been claimed for so long. This lie is maintained in order to get the population to agree to ever higher taxes and to cut off their cheap energy supply.

Even if the energy needs of humanity would stop increasing, our planet does not have enough land surface to build enough windmills and solar parks. Not to mention the gigantic load of steel and rare metals that would be needed, plus the fact that especially windmills have an extremely short lifespan (max. 20 years, practice shows that the first mills fail after just a few years. Cleaning up broken windmills is also a very costly affair).

Synthetic RNA and DNA are used to program people.

Musk is also a strong supporter of programmable (synthetic) RNA and DNA, which the Covid-19 vaccinations have already injected into a huge portion of the world's population. 'That reminds me of a computer program.' If you want to, you can probably stop and reverse the aging process with it.'

We have shown that the real goals of creating 'programmable' humans are much more sinister, and seem to be primarily aimed at totalitarian population and behavioral control, and massive population reduction.

Nevertheless, it is nice to hear for once a well-known top executive who has a positive view of humanity, something that can certainly not be said of the globalist climate-vaccine sect led by Klaus Schwab and Bill Gates.

Our other books

Check out our other books for other unreported news, exposed facts and debunked truths, and more.

Join the exclusive Rebel Press Media Circle!

You will get a new updates about the unreported reality delivered in your inbox every Friday.

Sign up here today:

https://campsite.bio/rebelpressmedia